THE BOOK OF CATHOLIC JOKES

D0062741

THE BOOK OF
CATHOLIC
JOKES

Deacon Tom Sheridan

Foreword by Father Gregory Sakowicz

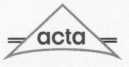
acta

THE BOOK OF CATHOLIC JOKES
by Deacon Tom Sheridan
with a Foreword by Father Gregory Sakowicz

Edited by Gregory F. Augustine Pierce
Editorial assistance by Mary Eggert and Donna Ryding
Cover design by Tom A. Wright
Text design and typesetting by Patricia Lynch

Published by ACTA Publications, 4848 N. Clark St., Chicago, IL 60640
(800) 397-2282, www.actapublications.com

Library of Congress Catalog number: 2008931393
ISBN: 978-0-87946-377-9
Printed in the United States of America by Total Printing Systems
Year 30 29 28 27 26 25 24 23 22 21 20 19
Printing 15 14 13 12 11 10 9 8 7

♻ Text printed on 30% post-consumer recycled paper

CONTENTS

FOREWORD
by Father Gregory Sakowicz

One time Groucho Marx stepped off a train in New York City and was greeted by a priest. "I want to thank you, Groucho, for all the joy and laughter you have brought into people's lives," the priest proclaimed.

"And I want to thank you, Father," Groucho replied, "for all the joy and laughter you have taken out of people's lives."

This is a "Catholic" joke, and it is funny. Why shouldn't religion—in this case the Catholic faith—celebrate the humor that is innate in the human condition? Why should Catholicism consider itself too pious to mine the rich vein of laughter that is surely a unique and irrepressible gift of a God who loves all human beings, despite our foibles and shortcomings and silliness?

A Catholic schoolteacher walks into her empty classroom one morning to find a note placed neatly upon her desk. The note reads simply: "If you are feeling okay today, please notify your face."

God must think the ability to make a joke is pretty special. After all, he apparently reserved this gift to us humans. Among all the creatures God has place on the earth, only we humans concoct jokes that can bring tears of laughter to our eyes. No other creature seems to see the wry humor behind a seemingly innocent comment or observation. Indeed, no other creature has the ability to make others laugh, chortle, cackle, chuckle, guffaw, giggle, snicker, snigger, snort or titter.

Two nuns are running away from a bear, who is gaining on them. "Do you think we'll be able to outrun him, Sister?" one of the nuns asks the other.

"I don't have to outrun him, Sister. I only have to outrun you," said the other nun.

They say it takes only fifteen muscles in our face to laugh, but it takes some seventy muscles to frown. This should give us some hint what the Creator has in mind for us most of the time. As the pastor of a wonderful Chicago parish, I find humor is a way of opening a window to my congregation's hearts and souls. Isn't that what Jesus did with his parables? Many were ironic and humorous comments on how we humans take ourselves too seriously and the ends we will go to get our own way. For example, he compared rich people to camels trying to get through the eye of a needle. He told the story of a relentless widow who simply wore down a judge until he ruled in her favor. He offered the ridiculous image of a gardener trying to spread manure around a dead fig tree in an attempt to get it to bear fruit. Yet these were all images of the kingdom of God, which was Jesus' main message. Apparently he thought that humor was an appropriate vehicle for religious instruction, so why should we be afraid of it?

A deacon and his wife invited their elderly pastor for Sunday dinner. While the couple was in the kitchen preparing the meal, the priest asked their son what they were having to eat.

"Goat," the little boy replied.

"Goat?" asked the startled man of the cloth. "Are you sure about that?

"Yep," said the youngster. "I heard Dad say to Mom before you came, 'Today is as good as any to have the old goat for dinner.'"

Humor is a learned experience. It starts when a little baby understands that hiding our face behind our hands and then saying "peek-a-boo" is funny, and it ends when we learn to kid one another about how old we are getting. One of the greatest sources of humor can be religion, for religion offers us an opportunity to laugh at ourselves at our most serious, and Jesus taught us that we shouldn't take ourselves all that seriously. "Unless you become like little children," he said, "you cannot enter the kingdom of heaven."

After receiving a beautiful haircut, a doctor asks the barber, "How much do I owe you?"

"Oh, I never charge a doctor," the barber replies. "You all do such good, important work."

The next morning, the barber arrives at his shop and finds a thank you note and a bottle of wine on his doorstep from the doctor.

Later that day, a police officer walks into the same barbershop. After a beautiful haircut, the police officer asks the barber, "How much to I owe you?"

"Oh, I never charge a police officer," the barber replies. "You all do such good, important work."

The next morning, the barber arrives at his shop and finds a thank you note and a box of candy on his doorstep from the police officer.

Later that day, a priest walks into the same barbershop. After a beautiful haircut, the priest asks the barber, "How much do I owe you?"

"Oh, I never charge a priest," the barber replies. "You all do such good, important work."

The next morning, the barber arrives at his shop and finds twelve priests on his doorstep.

I applaud my friend and colleague Tom Sheridan for assembling some very funny jokes (although sometimes they hit pretty close to home). This is a book of Catholic jokes because they are about Catholics or about Catholic practices, beliefs or customs. They reflect the Catholic incarnational sensibility that God is present in the everyday occurrences of daily life. But they are also "catholic" because they are for and about everyone, which is what "catholic" really means. Enjoy them, and don't be embarrassed to laugh out loud. Laughter is music for the soul!

ABOUT THESE JOKES

Catholic jokes fall into a couple of categories. Some are self-deprecating and let us laugh a little at ourselves. Others point out the human foibles of a supernatural church. Still others carry a little bit of irreverence or impiety. The rest are just plain funny, keying on some of the apparent absurdities of life.

Catholic humor is rich and varied. Some of the jokes in this book are no doubt familiar. Many you may never have heard before. Others have been adapted from what were originally secular or not specifically Catholic jokes. Though they've been collected from many sources, these jokes by no means form an exhaustive list of how we laugh at ourselves.

The Internet has made joke-sharing an art form. These jokes come from my own collection of jokes, from contributions of friends and colleagues, and from various websites and other publications. It's almost impossible to credit the origin of a specific joke—most have been circulation and evolving for years or even decades. Very few jokes have only a single source, and I believe these to be in the public domain. If authorship of a copyrighted joke has not been properly noted, please let the editors know and it will be corrected in subsequent editions.

Finally, we know there are hundreds or even thousands more good Catholic jokes. Everyone likely has a favorite. If yours is not included in this collection, and you'd like to submit one (or several) for possible inclusion in a followup edition, please write:

Deacon Tom Sheridan
The Book of Catholic Jokes
c/o ACTA Publications
actapublications@actapublications.com
www.actapublications.com

FAITH CAN BE FUNNY

A priest, a minister and a rabbi walk into a bar. The bartender is washing glasses. He looks up and says, "What is this, a joke?"

Actually, yes. That little one-liner is a pretty good example of how humor, perhaps especially religious humor, works. Humor takes an ordinary experience and twists it until it squeezes out a drop of laughter. Very often that drop turns into a gusher.

And sometimes there's even a dollop of wisdom.

Not all jokes are uproariously funny, you know. Many work with laughter on one hand, but offer a twist that gets us thinking.

One day a group of scientists got together and decided that man had come a long way and no longer needed God. So they picked one scientist to tell God that they were done with him.

The scientist walked up to God and said, "We've decided we no longer need you. We're to the point that we can clone people and do many miraculous things, so why don't you just go and get lost."

God listened patiently and said, "Very well, how about this? Let's say we have a man-making contest." The scientist replied, "Now you're talking! OK!"

God added, "We'll do it just like I did back in the old days."

"No problem," said the scientist, and bent down to grab a handful of dirt.

"No, no, no," said God. "Go get your own dirt!"

Or ...

Did you hear about the man standing before St. Peter at the Pearly Gates waiting to get into heaven? St. Peter asks what he did in life.

Proudly, the man says, "I was the president of a major HMO."

"In that case," St. Peter says, "you can come in for three days. Then you'll have to go to hell."

Or ...

Before celebrating a baptism, the deacon approached the young father and said solemnly, "Baptism is a serious step. Are you sure you're prepared for it?"

"I think so," the man replied. "My wife has made appetizers and we have a caterer coming to provide plenty of cookies and cakes for our guests."

"I don't mean that," the deacon said. "I mean, are you prepared spiritually?"

"Oh, sure," came the reply. "I've got a keg of beer and a case of whiskey."

It would be a mistake, though, to take such jokes too seriously. Still, if our shared faith can't stand up to a little ribbing, maybe it's not strong enough.

Faith may be serious business, but so is faithful laughter, which has been called the language of the soul. And, as one wag once reminded us, "Religion is too important to be taken seriously all the time."

This book is hardly deep theology, and some of the jokes might even be a little lame. But remember, even lame laughter is far better than no laughter at all. Humor is an emotion that connects us, breaks down barriers, heals divisions and acknowledges the presence of a God who has touched humanity.

It echoes the great Teilhard de Chardin who enthusiastically said: "Joy is the most infallible sign of the presence of God."

Plunge on, dear reader. See how Jesus—and the faith he launched—has sometimes been mischaracterized as stern and grim-faced rather than one like us who appreciated the foibles and humor of life.

Then, enjoy the jokes and—for God's sake—laugh!

THE JOKES

There's the story of the pastor and his deacon who were volunteering as carpenters to fix roofs for needy parishioners.

The deacon was on a ladder nailing. Each time he reached into his nail pouch and pulled out a nail, he'd look at it, and either toss it over his shoulder or nail it into the roof.

The pastor watched for a while, puzzled. Then he couldn't stand it any longer and yelled up, "Why are you throwing away some of the nails?"

The deacon explained, "When I pull it out of my nail pouch, if it's pointed toward me I throw it away. If it's pointed toward the house, then I can use it safely!"

The pastor became very frustrated at this and shouted, "That's stupid! Don't throw away the nails that are pointed toward you! They're for the other side of the roof!"

A laywoman goes to the post office to buy stamps for Christmas cards.

"I'd like 100 stamps," she says.

"What denomination?" asks the clerk.

"Oh, for Pete' s sake, has it really come to this?" complains the woman. "Well, OK, give me 50 Catholic, 10 Baptist, 20 Lutheran and 20 Presbyterian."

The new associate pastor, nervous about hearing confessions, asks an older priest to listen in. Several penitents later, his mentor offers a few suggestions.

"Cross your arms over your chest and rub your chin with one hand," he says. "Try saying things like, 'I see, yes, go on. I understand. How did you feel about that?'"

The new priest tries out the words and gestures. The old priest says, "Good, now, don't you think that's a little better than slapping your knee and saying, 'No way! You did *what*?'"

A boy asks his father to use the car and the father replies "No, not until you cut your hair!"

The boy replies, "But father…Jesus had long hair!"

"Yeah, but Jesus walked everywhere," said the father.

A little child in church for the first time watched as the ushers passed the offering plates. When they neared the pew where he sat, the youngster piped up so that everyone could hear: "Don't pay for me Daddy, I'm under five."

Catholic schoolchildren were asked questions about the Bible. The following have not been retouched or corrected for spelling.

In the first book of the Bible, Guinessis, God got tired of creating the world, so he took the Sabbath off.

Adam and Eve were created from an apple tree. Noah's wife was called Joan of Ark. Noah built an ark, which the animals come on to in pears.

Lot's wife was a pillar of salt by day, but a ball of fire by night.

The Jews were a proud people and throughout history they had trouble with the unsympathetic Genitals.

Samson was a strongman who let himself be led astray by a Jezebel like Delilah.

Moses led the hebrews to the Red Sea, where they made unleavened bread, which is bread without any ingredients.

The Egyptians were all drowned in the dessert. Afterwards, Moses went up on Mount Cyanide to get the ten ammendments.

The seventh commandment is thou shalt not admit adultery.

Moses died before he ever reached Canada. Then Joshua led the hebrews in the battle of Geritol.

The greatest miracle in the Bible is when Joshua told his son to stand still and he obeyed him.

David was a hebrew king skilled at playing the liar. he fought with the Finklesteins, a race of people who lived in Biblical times.

Solomon, one of David's sons, had 300 wives and 700 porcupines.

When Mary heard that she was the mother of Jesus, she sang the Magna Carta.

When the three wise guys from the east side arrived, they found Jesus in the manager.

Jesus was born because Mary had an immaculate contraption.

Jesus enunciated the Golden Rule, which says to do one to others before they do one to you. He also explained, "a man doth not live by sweat alone."

It was a miracle when Jesus rose from the dead and managed to get the tombstone off the entrance.

The people who followed the lord were called the 12 decibels. The epistles were the wives of the apostles.

One of the oppossums was St. Matthew who was also a taximan.

St. Paul cavorted to Christianity. He preached holy acrimony, which is another name for marriage.

Christians have only one spouse. This is called monotony.

Three men died and are at the Pearly Gates of heaven. St. Peter tells them that they can enter the gates if they can answer one simple question: "What is Easter?"

The first man replies, "Oh, that's easy, it's the holiday in November when everybody gets together, eats turkey, and is thankful...."

"Wrong!" says St. Peter sternly, and he turns to ask second man the same question.

He replies, "No, Easter is the holiday in December when we put up a nice tree, exchange presents and celebrate the birth of Jesus."

St. Peter shakes his head in disgust, looks at the third man and asks, "What is Easter?"

The third man smiles and looks St. Peter in the eye. "Of course I know what Easter is," he says. "Easter is the Christian holiday that coincides with the Jewish celebration of Passover. Jesus and his disciples were eating at the Last Supper and he was later deceived and turned over to the Romans by one of his disciples. The Romans made him wear a crown of thorns and he was hung on a cross and died. He was buried in a cave that was sealed off by a large boulder. Every year the boulder is moved aside so that Jesus can come out. And if he sees his shadow, there will be six more weeks of winter."

What do you call a nun who walks in her sleep?

A roaming Catholic.

A layman walked up to a Franciscan and a Jesuit and asked, "How many novenas must I say to get a Mercedes Benz?"

The Franciscan asked, "What's a Mercedes Benz?"

The Jesuit asked, "What's a novena?"

An Irish farmer named Muldoon lived alone in the countryside with a small dog that he loved and doted on. After many long years of faithful companionship, the dog finally died, so the farmer went to the parish priest and said, "Father, me dear old dog is dead. Could you be saying a Mass for him?"

The priest replied, "I'm so very sorry to hear about your dog's death. But unfortunately I can't say Mass for the poor creature."

Muldoon said, "I understand, Father, I do. I guess I'll go to that new denomination down the road; no tellin' what they believe. Do you think $500 is enough to donate for the service?"

The priest replied, "Why didn't you tell me that your dog was a Catholic?"

God is talking to one of his angels. He said, "Boy, I just created a 24-hour period of alternating light and darkness on Earth."

The angel replied, "What are you going to do now?"

God said, "Call it a day."

The Chief Rabbi of Israel and the Pope are meeting in Rome. The Rabbi notices an unusually fancy phone in the Pope's private chambers. "What's that phone for?" he asks.

"It's my direct line to the Lord," replies the Pope.

The Chief Rabbi is skeptical, and the Holy Father insists he try it out. Indeed the Rabbi is connected to the Lord and holds a lengthy discussion with him.

After hanging up the Chief Rabbi says, "Thank you very much. But I want to pay for my phone charges." The Pope, of course, refuses, but the Rabbi is steadfast, and finally the Pontiff gives in. He checks the counter on the phone and says, "The charges were $56." The Chief Rabbi gladly hands over the payment.

A few months later, the Pope is visiting Jerusalem. In the Chief Rabbi's chambers, he sees a phone like his and learns it is also is a direct line to the Lord. The Pope remembers he has an urgent matter that requires divine consultation and asks to use the Rabbi's phone. The Rabbi gladly agrees, hands him the phone, and the Pope chats away for twenty minutes.

After hanging up, the Pope offers to pay for the charges. Of course, the Chief Rabbi refuses, but after the Pope insists the Rabbi relents and looks up the charges. "The entire call was 42 cents," he says.

Surprised, the Pope asks, "Why so cheap?"

The Chief Rabbi smiles. "From here it's a local call," he says.

A middle-aged laywoman has a heart attack and is taken to the hospital. While on the operating table she has a near-death experience in which she sees God. She asks him if this is the end of her life. God tells her no, she has another 40 years to live.

After she recovers, she's so upbeat that she stays in the hospital and has a face-lift, liposuction, breast augmentation and a tummy tuck. She has a beautician come in to change her hair color and style. As long she's got another 40 years to live, she figures she might as well make the most of it.

The woman walks out the front door of the hospital after the last operation and is run over by an ambulance.

In front of God, she wails, "I thought you said I had another 40 years?"

God replies, "Sorry, I didn't recognize you."

A little boy was attending his first wedding. After the service, his cousin asked him, "How many women can a man marry?"

"Sixteen," the boy responded.

His cousin was amazed that he had an answer so quickly. "Wow! How do you know that?"

"Easy," the little boy said. "All you have to do is add it up, like the priest said: 4 better, 4 worse, 4 richer, 4 poorer."

A Brit, a Frenchman and a Russian are viewing a painting of Adam and Eve frolicking in the Garden of Eden.

"Look at their reserve, their calm," muses the Brit. "They must be British."

"Nonsense," says the Frenchman. "They're naked, and so beautiful. Clearly, they are French."

Then the Russian gets his say: "No clothes, no shelter. They have only an apple to eat and they're told this is paradise. No doubt they are Russian."

Did you know the apostles actually edited the Bible story about the woman caught in adultery because what really happened was quite awkward?

It seems Jesus was writing in the sand and said, "If any one of you is without sin, you be the first to throw a stone."

Suddenly, from out of nowhere, a rock came sailing in and whacked the poor woman in the head. Jesus stood up and with great exasperation said, "Mother!"

Photons have mass?
I didn't even know they were Catholic!

Catholic definitions:

CHOIR: A group of people whose singing allows the rest of the congregation to lip-sync.

HOLY WATER: A liquid whose chemical formula is H2OLY.

HYMN: A song of praise, usually sung in a key three octaves higher than that of the congregation's range.

INCENSE: Holy Smoke!

JESUITS: An order of priests known for their ability to found colleges with good basketball teams.

JONAH: The original "Jaws" story.

JUSTICE: When your children have kids of their own.

KYRIE ELEISON: The only Greek words that most Catholics can recognize besides gyros and baklava.

MAGI: The most famous trio to attend a baby shower.

MANGER:

> 1. Where Mary gave birth to Jesus because Joseph wasn't covered by an HMO.
>
> 2. The Bible's way of showing us that holiday travel has always been rough.

PEW: A medieval torture device still found in Catholic Churches.

PROCESSION: The ceremonial formation at the beginning of Mass, consisting of altar servers, the celebrant, and late parishioners looking for seats.

RECESSIONAL: The ceremonial procession at the conclusion of Mass—led by parishioners trying to beat the crowd to the parking lot.

RELICS: People who have been going to Mass for so long that they actually know when to sit, kneel, and stand.

TEN COMMANDMENTS: The most important Top Ten list not produced by David Letterman.

USHERS: The only people in the parish who don't know the seating capacity of a pew.

A little girl was sitting on her grandfather's lap as he read her a bedtime story. From time to time, she would take her eyes off the book and reach up to touch his wrinkled cheek. She was alternately stroking her own cheek, then his again. Finally she spoke up, "Grandpa, did God make you?"

"Yes, sweetheart," he answered, "God made me a long time ago."

"Oh," she paused, "Grandpa, did God make me too?"

"Yes, indeed, honey," he said, "God made you just a little while ago."

Feeling their respective faces again, the little girl observed, "God's getting better at it, isn't He?"

A couple of nuns were in the stands enjoying an exciting football game. Some rude guys sitting behind them decided to badger the sisters to get them to move.

One man says to others, loud enough for the nuns to hear, "I think I want to move to Utah. There are only 100 Catholics living there."

The second guy speaks up and says, "I want to go to Montana there are only 50 Catholics there."

The third guy jumps in with, "I want to go to Idaho, there are only 25 Catholics living there."

One of the nuns finally turns around and calmly says, "Why don't you all go to hell? There aren't any Catholics there."

———

A Jesuit was out for a drive and crashed into another car, only to discover that the other driver was a Franciscan.

"It was my fault," each insisted—as is only right and proper with religious men.

Concerned, the Jesuit said, "You look badly shaken up, Father. You could probably use a good stiff drink right now to calm down."

He produced a flask and the Franciscan drank from it and said, "Thank you, Father; I feel much better now. But you're probably shaken up too. Why don't you have a drink as well?"

"I will," the Jesuit replied, "but I think I'll wait until after the police have come."

A couple had two very mischievous little boys, ages eight and ten, who were always getting into trouble. The parents knew that if any mischief occurred in their town their sons were probably involved.

The boys' mother heard that a monsignor in town had been successful in disciplining children, so she asked if he would speak with her boys. The monsignor agreed. The mother sent the eight-year-old in first.

The monsignor, a huge man with a booming voice, sat the younger boy down and asked him sternly, "Where is God?"

The boy's mouth dropped open, but he made no response. He just sat there with his mouth hanging open, wide-eyed. So the monsignor repeated the question in an even stronger tone, "Where is God?" Again the boy made no attempt to answer.

So the monsignor raised his voice even more and shook his finger in the boy's face and bellowed, "WHERE IS GOD?"

The boy screamed and bolted from the room, ran directly home and dove into his closet, slamming the door behind him.

When his older brother found him, he asked, "What happened?"

The younger brother, gasping for breath, replied, "We are in BIG trouble this time, dude. God is missing—and they think WE did it!"

Paddy went into St. Mary's Hospital for major surgery. In the recovery room, the nurse came in and said, "So Pat, how will you be payin' for your surgery?"

"Sure and I don't know," said Pat.

"Do you have any insurance?" the nurse asked.

"No," said Pat.

"Do you have any money?" she asked.

"Not a penny," said Pat.

"Do you have any relatives who might be able to pay for this surgery?"

"Only me spinster sister in New Mexico; she's a nun.

"Nuns aren't spinsters Pat, they're married to God," the nurse said.

"Fine," replied Pat, "then sure and you'll be sending the bill to me Brother-in-Law."

The Catholic school teacher asks, "Now, Little Johnny, tell me honestly, do you say prayers before eating?" "No sir," Little Johnny replies, "I don't have to. My Mom is a good cook."

There's a guy at the Pearly Gates waiting to be admitted while St. Peter is paging through his book to see if the man is worthy. Peter flips through the book several times, furrows his brow, and says, "You know, I can't see that you did anything really good in your life but, you never did anything bad either. Tell you what, if you can tell me of one REALLY good deed that you did in your life, you're in."

The guy thinks for a moment and says, "Yeah, there was this one time when I was driving down the highway and I saw about 50 members of a biker gang torturing this poor dog. Infuriated, I got out my car, grabbed a tire iron and walked straight up to the gang's leader, a huge guy with a studded leather jacket and a chain running from his nose to his ear. As I walked up to the leader, his thugs circled around me. So I ripped the leader's chain off his face and smashed him in the head with the tire iron. Then I turned around and yelled to the rest of them, 'Leave this poor, innocent dog alone, you slime! Go home before I teach you all a lesson in pain!'"

St. Peter, impressed, says, "Really? When did this happen?"

"About two minutes ago," says the man.

To err is human, to moo bovine.

How many church people does it take to change a light bulb?

Charismatics: Only one. (His hands are already in the air.)

Roman Catholics: None. (They use candles.)

Baptists: Change?

Pentecostals: Ten. (One to change the bulb, nine to pray against the spirit of darkness.)

Presbyterians: None. (God has predestined when the lights will be on and off.)

Anglicans: Ten. (One to call the electrician, and nine to say how much they like the old bulb better.)

Mormons: Five. (One man to change the bulb, and four wives to tell him how to do it.)

Methodists: At least 15. (One to change the light bulb, and two or three committees to approve the change. Oh, and one to bring a casserole.)

Unitarians: (We choose not to make a statement either in favor for or against the need for light bulbs. However, if in your own journey, you have found a light bulb that works for you, that's fine. You are invited to write a poem or compose a modern dance about your personal relationship with your light bulb, and present it next month at our annual Light-bulb Sunday Service, in which we will explore a number of light-bulb traditions, including incandescent, fluorescent, three-way, long-life and tinted, all of which are equally valid paths to luminescence.)

In tears, Mary Clancy went up to Father O'Grady after the nine o'clock Mass.

He asks, "So what's bothering you, Mary my dear?"

She replies, "Oh, Father, I've got terrible news. My husband passed away last night."

The priest says, "Oh, Mary, that's terrible. Tell me, did he have any last requests?"

She says, "That he did, Father. He said, 'Please, Mary, put down that damn gun.'"

A young man is feeling ill and visits a doctor.

While he waits in the reception room, a nun comes out of the examination office. She's haggard and ashen.

When the man sees the doctor, he says, "I just saw that nun leaving; she looked absolutely terrible."

The doctor says, "I just told her she's pregnant."

The man exclaims: "Oh my, is she?"

"Of course not," says the doctor, "but it sure cured her hiccups."

During the wedding rehearsal, the groom approached the priest with an unusual offer. "Look, I'll give you $100 if you'll change the wedding vows. When you get to the part where I'm to promise to 'love, honor and obey' and 'forsaking all others, be faithful to her forever,' I'd appreciate it if you'd just leave that part out."

He slipped the priest the cash and walked away.

The wedding day arrived. When it came time for the groom's vows, the priest looked the young man in the eye and said, "Will you promise to prostrate yourself before her, obey her every command and wish, serve her breakfast in bed every morning of your life and swear eternally before God and your lovely wife that you will not ever even look at another woman, as long as you both shall live?"

The groom gulped and looked around and then said in a tiny voice, "I do."

After the ceremony, the groom pulled the priest aside and hissed, "I thought we had a deal."

The priest slipped the $100 back into the man's hand and whispered, "The bride's father made me a much better offer."

———

I think my karma just ran over your dogma.

A cop pulls over a car full of nuns. The cop says, "Sister, the speed limit on this highway is 55 mph. Why are you going so slow?"

Sister replies, "I saw a lot of signs that said 41, not 55."

The cop says, "Sister, that's the name of the highway, not the speed limit."

"Silly me," the embarrassed nun says, "Thanks for letting me know. I'll be more careful."

But then the cop glances in the back seat where the other nuns are quaking with fear. He asks, "Excuse me, Sister, what's wrong with your friends?"

Sister says, "Oh, we just got off Highway 101."

During a fire at a convent, a group of nuns are trapped on the third floor. Thinking quickly, they took off their habits, tied them together and used them as a rope to climb down from the window.

After safely reaching the ground, a reporter asks, "Weren't you worried that the habits would have ripped as you were climbing down? They look old and worn."

"Of course not!" said one of the nuns. "Don't you know how hard it is to break an old habit?"

There was a flood that threatened a village.

One man said to everyone, "I'm staying! God will save me!"

The flood started and a boat came by and the man in it said "Come on, get in!"

"No!" said the man. "God will save me!"

The waters kept rising and by now the man had climbed onto the roof.

A helicopter zoomed in and offered to rescue the man.

"No!" he said, "God will save me!"

Eventually, the man drowned.

At the gates of heaven, he expressed his disappointment to God: "Why didn't you save me?"

God said, "For goodness sake, child! I sent a boat and a helicopter. What more did you want?"

A priest and a rabbi met at the annual July 4th picnic. They were old friends and loved to tease one another.

"This baked ham is really good," said the priest. "You really ought to break down and try some."

"I will, I will," replies the rabbi, smiling, "at your wedding."

One Sunday morning, a priest saw a little boy staring intently at the large plaque on the church wall. The plaque was covered with names, and flags hung on either side of it.

"Father," asked the boy, "what's this?"

He replied, "It's a memorial to all the men and women who died in the service."

They stood together in silence for a moment. Finally, the boy asked with genuine concern: "Was it at the eight or the ten-thirty Mass?"

The catechist asked her Religious Education class to draw pictures of their favorite Bible stories. She was puzzled by one boy's picture, which showed four people on an airplane, so she asked him which story it was meant to represent.

"The flight to Egypt," he said.

"I see," said the catechist. "And that must be Mary, Joseph and Baby Jesus. But who's the fourth person?"

"Oh, that's Punches the Pilot."

As long as there are tests, there will be prayer in schools.

When Sister Marlena entered the Monastery of Silence, the Abbess said, "Sister, you have taken a vow of silence. You are welcome here as long as you like, but you may not speak unless I direct you to do so."

Five years later, the Abbess said to her, "Sister Marlena, you have been here for five years, you can speak two words." The nun looked at her superior and said, "Hard bed."

I'm sorry to hear about that," the Abbess said, "We will get you a better bed."

After another five years, the Abbess called Sister Marlena into her office. "You may say another two words, Sister."

"Cold food," said the nun.

The Abbess assured Sister Marlena that the food would be hotter in the future.

On her 15th anniversary at the monastery, Sister Marlena was again told by the Abbess, "You may say another two words today, Sister."

"I quit," said Sister Marlena.

"It's probably for the best," sighed the Abbess. "You've done nothing but complain since you got here."

———

Jesus is coming.

Look busy.

A bishop, a priest and a deacon, were about to be executed for preaching the Gospel in a foreign land.

They bring out the bishop first and the guard shouts, "Ready... aim..." and suddenly the bishop yells, "EARTHQUAKE." When everyone looks around, the bishop runs off.

Next they bring out the priest. The guard shouts, "Ready...aim..." and suddenly the priest yells, "TORNADO." When everyone ducks, the priest runs off.

By then, of course, the deacon had it figured out. They bring him out, and when the guard shouts, "Ready.... Aim...." Suddenly the deacon yells, "FIRE."

One day God looked at Earth and saw all kinds of evil going on.

So he sent a couple of angels down to check it out.

When they returned they said, "Lord, 95 percent of the people do not obey your will, and only 5 percent do."

God decided to e-mail the 5 percent who were good and encourage them.

Do you know what that e-mail said?

Oh, you didn't get a copy either?

An atheist was spending a quiet day fishing, when suddenly the Loch Ness monster attacked his boat. In one easy flip, the beast tossed the man and his boat at least a hundred feet into the air. It then opened its mouth, waiting below to swallow him whole. As the man started falling toward the open jaws of the ferocious beast, he cried out, "Oh, my God! Help me!"

Suddenly, the scene froze in place. As the atheist hung in mid-air, a booming voice came out of the clouds and said, "I thought you didn't believe in Me!"

"Come on, God, gimme a break!" the man pleaded. "Just seconds ago, I didn't believe in the Loch Ness monster either!"

"Well," said God, "now that you are a believer you must under-stand that I can't work a miracle just to save you from the jaws of the monster. But I can change hearts. What would you have me do?"

The atheist thinks fast and says, "God, please have the Loch Ness Monster believe in You also."

God replies, "So be it."

The scene is unfrozen and the atheist again begins falling toward the ravenous jaws of the monster. The monster folds his claws to-gether and says, "Lord, bless this food that You have so graciously provided...."

A preschool catechist was concerned that her students might be a little confused about Jesus Christ because of the Christmas season's emphasis on his birth. She wanted to make sure they understood that the birth of Jesus occurred a long time ago, that he grew up, and so forth.

So the teacher asked her class, "Where is Jesus today?"

Steven raised his hand and said, "He's in Heaven."

Mary called out, "He's in my heart."

Little Johnny, waving his hand furiously, finally blurted, "I know! I know! He's in our bathroom at home!"

The whole class became very quiet and looked at the teacher, who was completely at a loss for words. He finally gathered his wits and asked Johnny why he thought that Jesus was in his bathroom.

Johnny said, "Well, every morning, my father gets up, bangs on the bathroom door and yells, 'Jesus Christ, are you still in there?'"

A priest was giving a lesson on the 23rd Psalm to a group of children. He noticed that Little Johnny seemed upset by the verse, "Surely, goodness and mercy will follow me all the days of my life."

"What's wrong, Johnny?" the priest asked.

"Well," replied Little Johnny, "I'm not worried about goodness and mercy, but I'm not sure I'd like Shirley following me around all the time."

One day God and Adam were walking the garden. God told Adam that it was time to populate the Earth. "Adam, you can start by kissing Eve."

Adam looked puzzled at God, "Lord, what's a kiss?" God explained, and then Adam took Eve behind the bush and kissed her. A little while later, Adam returned with a big smile and said, "Lord! That was great! What's next?"

"Adam, I now want you to caress Eve." Puzzled again he asks, "Lord, what's a caress?" God explained, and then Adam took Eve behind the bush and caressed her. A little while later, Adam returned with a big smile and said, "Lord that was even better than a kiss! What's next?"

"Now I want you to make love to Eve," God said. Puzzled yet again, "Lord, what is making love?" asked Adam. God explained, and then Adam took Eve behind the bush. A few seconds later, Adam returned and asked, "Lord, what's a headache?"

A Sunday school teacher asked her little children, as they were on the way to church service, "And why is it necessary to be quiet in church?"

One little girl replied, "Because people are sleeping."

A rule of thumb for preachers:
If after ten minutes you haven't struck oil, stop boring!

One day Little Johnny asked his mother for a new bike. His mother said, "At Christmas you send a letter to Santa to ask for what you want, don't you?"

"Yes," replied Johnny, "but it isn't Christmas now."

His mother said, "Then you can send a letter to Jesus and ask him."

Johnny sat down with a pen and paper and started his letter: "Dear Jesus, I've been a good boy sometimes and I would like a new bike. Your Friend, Johnny."

He thought about this and decided to start over: "Dear Jesus, sometimes I think about being a good boy and I would like a new bike. Your Friend, Johnny."

He thought some more tried again: "Dear Jesus, someday I might be a good boy and I would like a new bike. Your Friend, Johnny."

Johnny didn't like that letter either. Finally, he got a small statue of Mary from the front yard and started his letter again: "Dear Jesus, if you ever hope to see your mother again, send me a new bike! Your Friend, Johnny."

A mother with a fidgety 7-year old boy told me how she finally got her son to sit still and be quiet. About halfway through the sermon, she leaned over and whispered, "If you don't be quiet, Father is going to lose his place and will have to start his sermon all over again!"

A rabbi and a priest were talking. The rabbi leans over and asked, "So how high can you advance in your organization?"

The priest said, "If I'm lucky, I guess I could become a bishop."

"Well, could you get any higher than that?" asked the Rabbi.

"I suppose that if my works are seen in a very good light that I might be made an archbishop," said the priest a bit cautiously.

"Is there any way that you might go higher?"

"If all the saints should smile, I guess I could be made a cardinal," mused the priest humbly.

"Could you be anything higher than a cardinal?" probed the rabbi.

Hesitating a little bit, the priest said, "Well, I suppose there's an outside chance I could be elected pope."

The rabbi continued to press, "Isn't there anything higher than pope you could become?"

"What! You think I could be Christ himself? I could never do that!" exclaimed the priest.

The rabbi leaned back and said, "Well, one of our boys already made it."

A layman finds himself in serious financial trouble. His business has gone bust and he decides to ask God for help. He begins to pray, "God, please help me. I've lost my business and if I don't get some money, I'm going to lose my house too. Please let me win the Lotto."

Lotto night comes, and somebody else wins it. The man prays harder. "God, please let me win the Lotto! I've lost my business, my house and now I'm going to lose my car."

Lotto night comes, and the man still has no luck. Once again, he prays, "My God, why have You forsaken me? I've lost my business, my house, and my car. My children are starving. I don't often ask You for help, and I have always been a good servant to You. PLEASE let me win the Lotto just this one time so I can get my life back in order."

Suddenly there is a blinding flash of light as the heavens open. The layman is overwhelmed by the voice of God Himself: "Hey, mister, work with Me on this. Buy one lousy ticket!"

After a church service on Sunday morning, a young boy suddenly announced to his mother, "Mom, I've decided to become a priest when I grow up."

"That's OK with us," she said, "but what made you decide that?"

"Well," said the little boy, "I have to go to church on Sunday anyway, and I figure it will be more fun to stand up and yell than to sit down and listen."

An engineer died and reported to the Pearly Gates. An intern angel, filling in for St. Peter, checked his dossier and grimly said, "Ah, an engineer; you're in the wrong place."

So the engineer was cast down to hell. Pretty soon, dissatisfied with the level of comfort hell offered, he began designing improvements. Soon, the underworld had air-conditioning, flush toilets and escalators. The engineer was becoming a pretty popular guy among the demons.

One day, God called Satan and asked, "So, how's it going down there in hell?"

Satan laughed and replied, "Hey, things are going great. We've got air-conditioning and flush toilets and escalators, and there's no telling what this engineer is going to come up with next."

God's face clouded over and he exploded, "What? You've got an engineer? That's a mistake; he should never have been there; send him up."

Satan shook his head, "No way. I like having an engineer down here. I've never had one before."

God was angry. "This isn't the way things are supposed to work and you know it. Send him back up here or I'll sue."

Satan laughed uproariously, "And just where are YOU going to get a lawyer?"

Walking along a California beach a laywoman was deep in prayer. Suddenly she cried out, "Lord, grant me one wish."

The sky darkened and a booming voice said, "Because you have had the faith to ask, I will grant you one wish."

The woman said, "I hate to fly, but I'd love to go to Hawaii. Please build a bridge to Hawaii so I can drive there whenever I want."

The Lord chastised the woman for such a selfish request and reminded her of the task's difficulty, saying, "Think of the logistics. Think of the supports required to reach the bottom of the Pacific! The concrete and steel it would take! I can do it, but it is hard for me to justify your desire for worldly things. Do you have another wish that would honor and glorify me."

The woman thought and said, "OK, Lord, I wish I could understand men. I want to know how they feel inside, what they're thinking, what they mean when they say 'nothing' is bothering them."

After a few minutes God said, "You want two lanes or four on that bridge?"

After creating heaven and earth, God created Adam and Eve. The first thing he said was, "Don't."

"Don't what?" Adam replied.

"Don't eat the forbidden fruit," God said.

"Forbidden fruit? We have forbidden fruit? Hey, Eve! We've got forbidden fruit!"

"No way!"

"Yes, way!"

"Do NOT eat the fruit!" commanded God.

"Why not?" said Adam.

"Because I am your Father and I said so!" God replied.

A few minutes later, God saw Adam and Eve having an apple break. He was angry and said, "Didn't I tell you not to eat the fruit?"

"Uh huh," Adam replied.

"Then why did you?" said the Father.

"I dunno," said Eve.

"She started it!" Adam said.

"Did not!"

"Did too!"

"DID NOT!"

Then God decided on Adam and Eve's punishment: They should have children of their own.

A parish administrator requested bids from local painters to re-paint the outside of the Pastoral Center. Almost all of the bids were within a few dollars of one another, with the exception of one by a parishioner who had been in business for years and had an excellent reputation in the community. This particular painter's bid was about half of his competitions, and naturally, the administrator accepted it.

On the day he was to begin, the painter realized that he had miscalculated badly. Not wanting to lose the job, however, he decided to thin the paint with water. That way, he thought, he would be able to complete the job for the price quoted.

A week later, he received a call from the administrator, complaining that after the first rain half of the paint had washed off the building. Being an honorable man and a good Catholic, the painter went inside to pray about the situation, knowing that his business' reputation was on the line.

"What can I possibly do, Lord?" prayed the discouraged painter.

In a loud voice God replied, "Repaint! Repaint and thin no more!"

A pastor got up one Sunday and announced to his congregation: "I have good news and bad news. The good news is we have enough money to pay for our new building program. The bad news is it's still out there in your pockets."

A laywoman who was taking a Scripture course discovered a burglar in her kitchen. Since she had no weapon to scare him off, she raised her hand and shouted, "Acts 2:38."

The burglar froze and didn't move, so the woman called 911. The police arrived and were amazed to find the burglar still frozen where he stood.

"What did you say to him?" they asked her.

She replied that she had just quoted scripture to him: "Repent, and be baptized every one of you in the name of Jesus Christ so that your sins may be forgiven."

As the cops put the burglar in the squad car, they asked him, "Why did her scripture verse scare you so much?"

"Scripture?" said the burglar, "I thought she said she had an axe and two 38s!"

The pastor was greeting folks at the door after the service. A woman said, "Father, that was a good sermon."

The priest replied, "Oh, I have to give the credit to the Holy Spirit."

"It wasn't THAT good!" she said.

The top 10 reasons God created Eve:

10. God was worried that Adam would become lost in the garden because he wouldn't ask for directions.

9. God knew that one day Adam would need someone to find the remote and hand it to him.

8. God knew Adam would never buy himself a new fig leaf. Or even know his size.

7. God knew Adam would never be able to make a doctor, dentist or haircut appointment for himself.

6. God knew Adam would never remember which night to put out the garbage.

5. God knew men would never be able to handle the pain and discomfort of childbearing.

4. As the garden's keeper, Adam would never remember where he left his tools.

3. Adam would need someone to blame his troubles on when God caught him hiding in the garden.

2. The Bible says, "It is not good for man to be alone," and the Bible is always right.

And finally, the No. 1 reason why God created Eve:

1. When God finished making Adam, He stepped back and said, "I can do better than that."

Did you know that in Las Vegas there are more churches than casinos?

Not surprisingly, chips sometimes end up in the collection basket. Since the churches get chips from many different casinos, they've devised a method to collect the offerings.

The churches send their chips to a nearby Franciscan monastery for sorting and then the chips are taken to the right casino to be cashed in.

You know who does this?

The chip monk, of course.

A homeless man, down on his luck, went into a Catholic church that was known for its rather "uppity" social reputation. Spotting the man's dirty clothes, the ushers stopped him outside the church door and asked if he needed help. The man told them, "I was praying and the Lord told me to come to this church."

The ushers suggested that the man go away and pray some more and he might get a different answer.

The following Sunday the man returned and the ushers again stopped him at the door. "Well, did you get a different answer?" they asked him.

"Yes, I did," said the man. "I told the Lord that you don't want me here, but the Lord said, 'Keep trying, son. I've been trying to get into that church for years and I haven't made it yet either.'"

One day an inebriated Catholic ice fisherman drilled a hole in the ice and peered into it when a loud voice rang out from above, "There are no fish there."

The man walked several yards and drilled another hole. Again, the voice boomed out, "There are no fish there."

Then the man stumbled 50 yards away and drilled another hole. For the third time, the voice yelled, "I told you, there are no fish there."

Finally, the fisherman looked up into the sky and asked, "God, is that you?"

"No, you idiot," the voice said, "I'm the skating rink manager."

A young layman was climbing a cliff when suddenly he slipped. He grabbed a branch and hung there. He couldn't pull himself up and was becoming exhausted. Finally he looked up to the heavens and cried out: "God, help me; please, help me."

Suddenly the clouds parted and a deep voice resounded, "Let go!"

The young man paused, looked around, and then he looked up at heaven once more and said: "Is anyone else up there?"

An atheist was complaining to a Catholic friend, "Christians have their special holidays, like Christmas and Easter, Jews have Passover and Yom Kippur. Even Muslims have their holidays. EVERY religion has its holidays. But we atheists have no holidays. It's unfair discrimination."

"What do you mean, atheists have no holidays?" the friend said. "People have been observing a special day in your honor for years."

"What do you mean?" the atheist asked. "When is there a special day honoring atheists?"

"Every April 1," said the friend.

A priest is driving down a highway when a state trooper stops him for speeding.

The trooper smells alcohol on the priest's breath and spots an empty wine bottle rolling around on the floor of the car. He says, "Father, have you been drinking?"

The priest replies, "Just water."

The trooper asks, "Then why do I smell wine?"

The priest looks down at the bottle and says, "Good Lord, He's done it again!"

Three friends die in a car crash, and they find themselves at the Gates of Heaven. Before entering, St. Peter asks each of them a question.

"When you are in your casket and friends and family are standing there mourning you, what would you like to hear them say about you?" asks St. Peter.

The first guy says, "I would like to hear them say that I was a great doctor and a great family man."

The second guy says, "I would like to hear that I was a wonderful husband and a teacher who made a huge difference in our children."

The last guy replies. "I would like to hear them say: 'LOOK! HE'S STILL MOVING!'"

A laywoman was driving down the street in a sweat because he had an important meeting and couldn't find a parking place. Looking up toward heaven, she said, "Lord, take pity on me. If you find me a parking place I'll go to Mass every Sunday for the rest of my life and give up drinking wine."

Miraculously, a parking place opened up right in front of her destination.

The woman looked up to heaven again and said, "Never mind, Lord; I found one on my own."

A priest was finishing up a homily about temperance. With great expression he said, "If I had all the beer in the world, I'd take it and throw it into the river!"

The congregation nodded approval and shouted, "Amen."

"And if I had all the whiskey in the world," said the priest, "I'd take it and throw it into the river!"

The congregation said again, "Amen!"

As the priest sat down, the music minister stood and announced, "For our closing song, let us sing hymn 365: Shall We Gather at the River."

And the congregation all sang, "Amen."

———

A layman is talking to God and asks, "Hey, God, what does 100 million years seem like to you?"

God answered, "One hundred million years? That's like a second to me."

Then the man asks, "So what's $100 million seem like to you?"

"One hundred million dollars?" says God. "It seems like a penny to me."

So the man says, "Hey, God, could I borrow a penny?"

And God replies, "Sure. Just wait a second."

Little Johnny wanted $100 for a new bike and prayed for two weeks, but nothing happened.

Then he decided to write God a letter asking for the money. When the local postmaster saw the letter addressed to "God, USA," he decided to send it to the President of the United States.

The President was so impressed, touched and amused that he instructed his secretary to send the little boy a $5 bill.

Little Johnny was delighted with the $5 and wrote a thank-you note to God. It read: "Dear God, thank you for sending the money. However I noticed that for some reason you had to send it through Washington, D.C. As usual, those crooks deducted $95."

Little Johnny opened the big family Bible with fascination, and looked through the old pages.

Suddenly, something fell out of the Bible. Little Johnny picked it up and looked. An old leaf from a tree had been pressed between the pages. "Momma, look what I found," he called out.

"What have you got there, dear?" his mother asked.

With astonishment in the young boy's voice, he answered: "I think it's Adam's swim suit!"

Two bishops died at the same time and met St. Peter at the Pearly Gates. St. Peter said, "I'd like to get you guys in now, but our computer is down. You'll have to go back to Earth for about a week, but you can't go back as bishops. So what else would you like to be?"

The first bishop says, "I've always wanted to be an eagle, soaring above the Rocky Mountains."

"So be it," says St. Peter, and off flies the first bishop.

The second bishop thinks for a minute and asks, "Will this week count against us in any way, St. Peter?"

"No," said Peter. "I told you, the computer's down. There's no way we can keep track of what you're doing."

"In that case," said the second bishop, "I've always wanted to be a stud."

"So be it," said St. Peter.

A week goes by, the computer is fixed, and the Lord tells St. Peter to recall the two bishops. "Will you have any trouble locating them?" God asks.

"The first one should be easy," says St. Peter. "He's somewhere over the Rockies, flying with the eagles. But the second one could prove to be more difficult."

"Why?" asked the Lord.

"He's on a snow tire, somewhere in North Dakota."

A driver tucked a note under her windshield wiper: "I've circled the block for 20 minutes. I'm late for an appointment, and if I don't park here I'll lose my job. Forgive us our trespasses."

Returning, she came back to find a parking ticket and another note: "I've circled the block for 20 years, and if I don't give you a ticket I'll lose my job. Lead us not into temptation."

A friend was in front of me coming out of church one day, and the pastor was standing at the door to shake hands. He grabbed my friend by the hand and pulled him aside and said, "You need to join the Army of the Lord!"

My friend replied, "I'm already in the Army of the Lord, Father."

"If that's true," said the pastor, "how come I only see you on Christmas and Easter?"

My friend whispered back, "I'm in the Secret Service."

How long should a good homily be?

It should be like a woman's skirt:
long enough to cover the essentials
and short enough to keep you interested.

An old priest was dying. He sent a message for a banker and a lawyer, both parishioners, to come to his home.

They were ushered up to his bedroom in the rectory. The preacher held out his hands and motioned for them to sit on each side of the bed. Grasping their hands, he sighed contentedly, smiled, and stared at the ceiling. For a time, no one said anything.

Both the banker and lawyer were flattered that the preacher would ask them to be with him during his final moments. They were also puzzled; the preacher had never given them any indication that he particularly liked either of them. They both remembered his many uncomfortable sermons about greed, covetousness and avaricious behavior that made them squirm in their seats.

Finally, the banker said, "Father, why did you ask us to come?"

The old priest mustered up his strength and then said weakly, "Jesus died between two thieves, and that's how I want to go."

———

The little church suddenly stopped buying from its regular office supply dealer. So the dealer phoned the pastor to ask why.

"I'll tell you why," shouted the pastor indignantly. "Our church ordered some pencils from you to be used in the pews for visitors to register."

"Well," interrupted the dealer, "didn't you receive them yet?"

"Oh, we received them all right," replied the pastor. "You sent us little pencils each stamped with the words: Play Golf Next Sunday."

Three boys were bragging about their fathers. The first boy says, "My dad is a poet. He scribbles a few words on a piece of paper, calls it a poem, and they give him $50."

The second boy says, "That's nothing. My dad is in advertising. He scribbles a few words on a piece of paper, calls it a song, and they give him $100."

The third boy says, "I've got you both beat. My dad is a deacon. He scribbles a few words on a piece of paper, calls it a homily, and it takes eight people to collect all the money!"

———

A priest, known for his lengthy homilies, noticed a man get up and leave during the middle of his message. The man came back just before the end of Mass. Afterward the priest asked the man where he had gone.

"I went to get a haircut," was the reply.

"But," said the priest, "why didn't you do that before the service?"

"Because," the man said, "I didn't need one then."

———

A catechist asked her class why Joseph and Mary took Jesus with them to Jerusalem.

A small child replied, "They couldn't get a baby-sitter?"

There once was a rich layman who was near death. He was very upset because he had worked so hard for his money and wanted to be able to take it with him to heaven. So he prayed that he might be able to keep some of his wealth.

An angel heard his plea and appeared to him. "Sorry, but you can't take your wealth with you."

The man begged the angel to speak to God to see if He might bend the rules. The angel reappeared and informed the dying man that God had decided to allow him to take one suitcase. Overjoyed, the man gathered his largest suitcase and filled it with pure gold bars.

He died soon afterward and showed up at the gates of heaven.

St. Peter saw the suitcase and stopped the man, but he explained that he had God's OK.

St. Peter checked it out and said, "You're right; you're allowed one carry-on bag, but I'm supposed to check its contents."

St. Peter opened the case to inspect the items that the man found too precious to leave behind and exclaimed, "You brought more pavement?"

A six-year-old was overheard reciting the Lord's Prayer at a church service: "And forgive us our trash passes, as we forgive those who passed trash against us."

Sister Mary, who worked for a home health agency, was out making her rounds visiting homebound patients when she ran out of gas. As luck would have it, a gas station was just a block away.

She walked to the station to borrow a gas can and buy some gas. The attendant told her the only gas can he owned had been loaned out but she could wait until it was returned. Since the nun was on the way to see a patient, she decided not to wait and walked back to her car. She looked for something in her car that she could fill with gas and spotted the bedpan she was taking to the patient. Always resourceful she carried the bedpan to the station, filled it with gas, and carried the full bedpan back to her car.

As she was pouring the gas from the bedpan into her tank, two men watched from across the street. One turned to the other and said, "If that thing starts, I'm turning Catholic!"

Everybody knew the church roof was leaking, but the parish kept putting off replacement because repairs would cost tens of thousands of dollars.

Finally, when the ceiling began to sag, the parish council called an emergency meeting of the entire congregation. A wealthy parishioner stood up and pledged $300 toward fixing the roof. Just then a small piece of the ceiling fell and hit him on the head.

Somebody in the back of the church said, "Hit him again, Lord!"

One Sunday morning a mother was getting ready for church when she noticed her son wasn't up yet. She finally went in to wake him up. "Come on, get up. You'll be late for Mass!" she said.

"I don't want to go!" said her son as he buried his head under the pillow.

"You have to go," the mother coaxed.

"No, I'm not going," he insisted. "And I'll give you two reasons. Nobody there likes me and I don't like them."

Indignantly, his mother replied, "You are too going to church, and I'll give you two reasons: You're 45 years old and you're the pastor!"

———

The story of Adam and Eve was being carefully explained in the children's religious education class. Following the story, the children were asked to draw some picture that would illustrate what happened.

Little Johnny drew a picture of a car with three people in it. In the front seat, behind the wheel was a man and in the back seat, a man and a woman.

The teacher didn't understand how this illustrated the lesson of Adam and Eve. But Little Johnny explained: "Why, this is God driving Adam and Eve out of the garden!"

There's a little old Catholic lady living next door to an atheist. Every morning the lady goes out on her front porch and shouts, "Praise the Lord!"

And every day, the atheist yells back, "There is no God!"

After a while, though, the lady runs into financial difficulties and has trouble buying food. But every morning she goes out on the porch and asks God for help with groceries and then shouts, "Praise the Lord!"

One morning when she goes out on her porch, she discovers the groceries she's prayed for, of course she shouts "Praise the Lord!"

Just then, the atheist leaps out from behind a bush and says, "Ha, there's no God—I bought those groceries for you!"

The lady looks at him and smiles. Then she shouts all the louder, "Praise the Lord! Not only did you provide for me, Lord, you also made Satan pay for the groceries!"

———

They even have Dial-a-Prayer for atheists now.

It rings and rings but nobody answers.

The catechist asked her class of seven-year-olds, "If I sold my house and my car, had a big garage sale and gave all my money to the church, would that get me into heaven?"

"NO!" answered all the children.

"If I cleaned the church every day, mowed the yard and kept every thing neat and tidy, would that get me into heaven?"

Again, they answered, "NO!"

"Well, then, if I was kind to animals and gave candy to all the children, and loved my husband, would that get me into heaven?"

Again, they all answered, "NO!"

Perplexed, the woman continued, "Then how can I get into heaven?"

One of the boys shouted out, "YOU GOTTA BE DEAD!"

A pastor was opening his mail one morning and one envelope had only a single sheet of paper with a single word printed on it: "FOOL!"

The following Sunday the priest announced, "I have known many people who have written letters and forgotten to sign their name. But this week I received a letter from someone who signed his name and had forgotten to write a letter."

Gallagher opened the morning newspaper and was dumbfounded to read in the obituary column that not only had he died but also the local church had already scheduled his funeral Mass. He quickly phoned his best friend Finney.

"Finney, did ye see the paper?" asked Gallagher. "Sure and they say I died!"

"Sure and I saw it!" replied Finney. "Where are ye callin' from?"

The children were all lined up for their first confession when Little Johnny's turn came. The priest asked him to confess his sins, and the boy promptly replied "Father, I threw a stone at Jimmy."

"That was a very misguided thing to do, my son," said the priest patiently.

"It wasn't misguided at all," said Little Johnny. "I hit him."

Little Susie was watching her father the deacon write a homily.

"How do you know what to say?" she asked her dad.

"Why, God tells me."

"Then why do you keep crossing things out?"

After Quasimodo's death, the bishop of the Cathedral of Notre Dame sent word throughout Paris that a new bell-ringer was needed. The bishop decided that he would conduct the interviews in the belfry. Several applicants demonstrated their skills, when a lone, armless man came in and said he was there to apply for the bell-ringer's job.

The incredulous bishop said, "But you have no arms!"

"No matter," said the man, "Observe!" He then began striking the bells with his face, producing a beautiful melody. The astonished bishop listened and knew he had found a suitable replacement for Quasimodo.

But suddenly, the armless man tripped, and plunged out the belfry window to his death.

When the stunned bishop reached the street, a crowd had gathered around the fallen figure, drawn by the beautiful music they had heard only moments before. One of them asked, "Bishop, who was this man?" "I don't know his name," the bishop sadly replied, "but his face rings a bell."

Despite the sad event, the bishop continued his interviews for the bell-ringer of Notre Dame. The first applicant said, "Your Excellency, I am the twin brother of the poor, armless wretch who fell to his death from this very belfry yesterday. I pray that you honor his life by allowing me to replace him in this duty."

The bishop agreed to give the man an audition, but as he prepared to ring the bells the man groaned, clutched at his chest and died on the spot. Two monks, hearing the bishop's cries of grief at this second tragedy, rushed up the stairs to his side. "What has happened?," the first monk asked breathlessly, "Who is this man?"

"I don't know his name," sighed the distraught bishop, "but he's a dead ringer for his brother."

The 98-year-old Mother Superior from Ireland was dying.

The nuns gathered around her bed trying to make her last journey comfortable. They tried to give her some warm milk to drink but she refused. One of the nuns took the glass back to the kitchen where she remembered the bottle of Irish whiskey received as a gift the previous Christmas. She poured a generous amount into the warm milk.

Back at Mother Superior's bed, she held the glass to her lips. Mother sipped a little, then a little more, and before they knew it she had drunk the whole glass.

"Mother," the nuns asked with earnest, "please give us some wisdom before you die."

She raised herself up in bed and with a pious look on her face said, "Whatever you do, don't sell that cow!"

What do you get if you cross a Jehovah's Witness and a Unitarian?

Someone who goes around knocking on doors
for no apparent reason.

Karl Rahner, Hans Kung and Pope Benedict XVI all die on the same day and go to meet St. Peter to learn their fate.

St. Peter says he'll interview each of them to discuss their views on various theological issues. He points at Rahner and says "Karl! In my office." Four hours later, the door opens, and Rahner comes stumbling out. He is highly distraught and mumbles, "Oh God, that was the hardest thing I've ever done! How could I have been so wrong! So sorry…. I never knew…." He stumbles off into Heaven, a testament to God's mercy.

St. Peter follows him out, and points his finger in Kung's direction and says, "Hans! You're next." Eight hours later, the door opens, and Kung comes out, barely able to stand. He is near collapse with weakness and a crushed spirit. He, too, is mumbling, "Oh God, that was the hardest thing I've ever done! How could I have been so wrong! So sorry…. I never knew…." He stumbles off into Heaven, a testament to God's mercy.

Finally, St. Peter says, "Benedict, your turn." Twelve hours later, St. Peter stumbles out, exhausted, saying, "Oh God, that was the hardest thing I've ever done. How could I have been so wrong! So sorry…. I never knew…."

How cold was it the other day?

So cold the diocesan director of development
had his hands in his own pockets.

Three pastors from neighboring parishes were having lunch at a diner.

The first said, "You know, since the summer started I've been having a lot of trouble with bats in the loft and attic of my church. I've tried everything—noise, spray, cats—nothing seems to scare them away."

The second pastor replied, "Me too. I've got hundreds of those things living in my bell tower and in the narthex attic. I had the whole place fumigated, but they still won't go away."

The third said, "I had that problem a while ago. So I baptized all the bats and haven't seen one back since!"

Paddy was visiting New York City for the first time. He was waiting patiently to cross Fifth Avenue.

The traffic cop kept stopping the traffice and shouting, "OK, pedestrians, you can cross now." But Paddy didn't move.

After this happened several times, Paddy had finally had enough. He went up to the cop and said, "Sure and it's about time, Officer, that ye let the Cat'lics cross!"

A newly ordained deacon was asked to hold a graveside service for someone with no family or friends. It was his first official assignment, so he eagerly agreed.

Taking his duties very seriously, the deacon left early the next morning for the cemetery. However, he made several wrong turns and quickly got himself lost. When he finally arrived more than an hour late, the hearse was nowhere to be seen and the two workmen were eating lunch.

The deacon got out of his car, quickly threw on his vestments, and hurried to the open grave. Looking into the pit, he saw that the vault lid was already in place. With a sigh, he took out his prayer book and read the burial service.

After he had left, one of the workmen said to the other, "Maybe we should have told him he just blessed a septic tank."

Saints Dominic, Francis of Assisi and Ignatius of Loyola are transported back in time and place to the birth of Our Lord.

St. Dominic, seeing the Incarnation of the Word, is sent into ecstasy.

St. Francis, seeing God become a helpless child, is overcome with humility.

St. Ignatius of Loyola takes Mary and Joseph aside and asks, "Have you given any thought to his education?"

There was a barber who paid close attention at his parish whenever the topic of evangelization was discussed. He thought he should be doing more to share his faith with his customers.

The next morning the barber told the Lord in prayer, "Today I'm going to witness to the first customer who walks through my door."

A man came in as he opened his shop and said, "I need a shave." The barber said, "Yes sir! Just have a seat and I'll be right with you." The barber went in the back and prayed a quick prayer saying, "Lord, the first customer just came in and I'm going to witness to him. Give me the wisdom to know just the right thing to say. Amen."

Then the barber came out with his straight razor in one hand and a Bible in the other and told his customer: "I have a question for you: Are you ready to meet your Maker?"

The children were lined up in the cafeteria of a Catholic elementary school for lunch. At the head of the table was a large pile of apples. There was a note posted by the fruit. "Take only one," it read." God is watching."

At the other end of the line was a large pile of chocolate chip cookies. One child whispered to another, "Take all you want. God's watching the apples."

A four-year-old boy was asked to give thanks before Christmas dinner. The family members bowed their heads in expectation.

He began his prayer by thanking God for all his friends, naming them one by one. Then he thanked God for Mommy, Daddy, brother, sister, Grandma, Grandpa, and all his aunts and uncles.

Finally, he began to thank God for the food. He gave thanks for the turkey, the dressing, the fruit salad, the cranberry sauce, the pies, the cakes, even the Cool Whip. Then he paused, and everyone waited and waited. After a long silence, the young fellow looked up at his mother with a concerned look and asked, "If I thank God for the broccoli, won't He know that I'm lying?"

Little Johnny was in a relative's wedding. As he was coming down the aisle, he would take two steps, stop, and then turn to the crowd, put his hands up like claws and roar.

That's the way it went all down the aisle: step, step, ROAR…step, step, ROAR…step, step, ROAR.

As you can imagine, the crowd was near tears from laughing by the time he reached the pulpit. When the priest who was celebrating the wedding asked what he was doing, Little Johnny sniffed and said, "I was being the Ring Bear."

A religious education class was almost finished making their models of the nativity scene and one little boy had done a lovely job. Some animals, Mary, Joseph, three wise men, shepherds were all there. However the teacher noticed an extra, rather overweight man in the scene as well.

"Who is that person?" she asked.

"Oh, that's Round John Virgin."

Three preachers sat discussing the best positions for prayer while a telephone repairman worked nearby.

"Kneeling is definitely best," claimed one.

"No," another contended. "I get the best results standing with my hands outstretched to heaven."

"You're both wrong," the third insisted. "The most effective prayer position is lying prostrate, face down on the floor."

The repairman could contain himself no longer. "Hey, fellas," he interrupted, "the best prayin' I ever did was hangin' upside down from a telephone pole."

The six-year-old girl and her four-year old brother were sitting together at Mass. The boy couldn't keep quiet. He giggled, sang and talked out loud.

Finally, his big sister had had enough. "You're not supposed to talk at Mass."

"Why? Who's going to stop me?" the boy asked.

She pointed to the back of the church and said, "See those men standing by the door? They're hushers."

———

Dear Lord, so far today I've done all right: I haven't gossiped; lost my temper; been greedy, grumpy, nasty, selfish or overindulgent.

I'm very thankful for the kind of day You have given me.

But in a few minutes, Lord, I'm going to get out of bed, and from then on I'm going to need a lot more help. Amen.

———

A boy walked up to the pastor after Mass and handed him a dollar. The priest told him he should give it to the poor. "That's why I gave it to you, Father, because my dad says you're the poorest preacher we ever had."

At dinner in the rectory one night, the old pastor said to his new young associate, "Yes, it was a good idea to replace the first four pews with plush bucket theatre seats. Worked like a charm. Now the front of the church always fills up first."

The young priest beamed at the praise as the old priest continued, "And you said more beat to the music would bring young people back to church, so I supported you when you brought in that rock 'n roll gospel choir. Now we're packed to the balcony!"

"Thank you, Father," replied the young priest. "I'm pleased that you're open to the new youthful ideas."

"However," said the elderly priest, "You did go too far with the drive-thru confessional."

"But, Father," protested the young priest, "my confessions and the donations have nearly doubled!"

"I know, my son," replied the elderly priest, "but that flashing neon sign, 'Toot 'n Tell or Go to Hell' cannot stay on the church roof!"

A catechist was discussing the Ten Commandments with her six-year-olds. After explaining the commandment to "honor thy father and thy mother," she asked, "Is there a commandment that teaches us how to treat our brothers and sisters?"

Without missing a beat, one little boy answered, "Thou shall not kill."

Two Jewish fathers, long-time friends, happened to meet. One seemed depressed.

"What's wrong?" the other asked

"There's terrible trouble in my family," the first man said. "I sent my son to Israel so that he would come home a better Jew, and believe it or not he came home a Catholic."

"Funny you should mention that," said the second man. "Exactly the same thing happened to my son. I sent him to Israel in hope that he would become a better Jew, and believe it or not he also came home a Catholic."

Together, they decided to seek the advice of their rabbi. He responded, "Funny you should mention that," said the rabbi, "because exactly the same thing happened in our family. I sent my only son to Israel in hope that he would become a better Jew, and believe it or not he also came home a Catholic."

The three men fell to their knees and with tears streaming down their faces, crying their troubles out to God. Finally, they heard a voice from heaven: "Funny you should mention that...."

———

A father was reading Bible stories to his young son: "Lot was warned to take his wife and flee from the city, but his wife looked back and was turned into a pillar of salt."

The son asked, "But what happened to the flea?"

Recently a teacher, a garbage collector and a lawyer wound up together at the Pearly Gates. St. Peter informed them that in order to get into heaven, they would each have to answer one question.

St. Peter addressed the teacher and asked, "What was the name of the ship that crashed into the iceberg? They just made a movie about it." The teacher answered quickly, "That would be the Titanic." St. Peter let her through the gate.

St. Peter turned to the garbage man and, figuring heaven didn't REALLY need all the odors this guy would bring with him, decided to make the question a little harder: "How many people died on the ship?" But the trash man had just seen the movie, too, and he answered, "about 1,500."

"That's right! You may enter," said Peter.

Then St. Peter turned to the lawyer and said, "Name them."

———

Adam was returning home late one night. When Eve confronted him. "You're seeing another woman, aren't you?" she accused.

"Don't be silly," he replied. "You're the only woman on earth."

Later that night Adam felt a tickle and woke up. "What are you doing, Eve?" he demanded.

"I'm counting your ribs," she said.

The pastoral associate, the associate pastor and the pastor are taking a shortcut to a meeting. As they walk through a vacant lot, the trio stumbles on an ancient oil lamp. On a lark they rub it, and to their amazement a genie appears and offers to grant them each one wish.

The pastoral associate cries out, "I want to be on an island paradise, lolling in the sun without a care!" The genie waves his hand and she disappears in a puff of smoke.

The associate pastor jumps up and says, "I want to be walking through the halls of the Vatican, marveling at all the artwork and never have to go to another meeting as long as I live." He too disappears.

Scowling, the pastor says to the genie, "I want those two back in time for the meeting."

Each year at the beginning of religion education classes, a veteran teacher sends this note to all parents: "If you promise not to believe everything your child says happens at class, I'll promise not to believe everything he or she says happens at home."

Did you know that they had automobiles in Jesus' time?

Yes, the Bible says that the disciples were all of one Accord.

After the christening of his baby brother in church, Little Johnny cried all the way home in the back seat of the car. His father asked him what was wrong and finally, the boy sobbed, "That priest said he wanted us brought up in a Christian home, and I want to stay with you guys!"

Did you hear the one about the man who opened a dry-cleaning business next door to the convent? He knocked on the door and asked the Mother Superior if she had any dirty habits.

In the beginning, God created the heavens and the earth, and then He rested.

Then God created man, and then they both rested.

Then God created woman, and since then neither God nor man has ever rested.

How did the bishop make holy water?

He took some tap water and boiled the hell out of it.

After 60-plus years of marriage, an 85-year-old couple dies in a car crash. They had been in good health the last ten years mainly due to her interest in health food and exercise.

When they reached the Pearly Gates, St. Peter took them to their mansion that was decked out with a beautiful kitchen and master bath suite and Jacuzzi.

As they oohed and aahed, the old man asked Peter how much all this was going to cost.

"It's free," Peter replied, "this is heaven."

Next they went out back to survey the championship golf course that the home backed up to. They would have golfing privileges every day.

The old man asked, "What are the green fees?"

Peter's reply, "This is heaven, you play for free."

Next they went to the clubhouse and saw the lavish buffet lunch with the cuisine of the world laid out.

"How much does it cost to eat?" asked the old man.

"Don't you understand yet? This is heaven; it is free!" Peter replied with exasperation.

"Well, where are the low-fat and low-cholesterol tables?" the old man asked timidly.

Peter lectured, "That's the best part. You can eat as much as you like of whatever you like and you never get fat and you never get sick. This is heaven."

With that the old man went into a fit of anger, shrieking wildly.

His wife tried to calm him down, but the old man looked at her and yelled, "If it weren't for you making me eat all those blasted bran muffins, I could have been here ten years ago!"

Little Jonnie was coming home from church one Sunday morning with his mother. His mother noticed he had a very serious look on his face.

"What's on your mind, Jonnie?" she asked.

"Is it true what Father said about us all coming from dust and turning back to dust?"

"Yes, it is, Jonnie," she said. "Why do you ask?"

"Well, when we get home," he answered, "You better look under my bed, because someone's either comin' or goin'!"

After the fall, Adam was walking with his sons Cain and Abel. As they were passing the locked gates of the Garden of Eden, one of the boys asked, "What's that?"

Adam replied, "Boys, that's where your mother ate us out of house and home."

A newly discovered chapter in the Book of Genesis has provided the answer to "Where do pets come from?"

Adam said, "Lord, when I was in the garden, you walked with me everyday. Now I don't see you anymore. I'm lonesome here and it's difficult for me to remember how much you love me."

And God said, "No problem! I will create a companion for you that will be with you forever and who will be a reflection of my love for you, so that you will love me even when you cannot see me. Regardless of how selfish or childish or unlovable you may be, this new companion will accept you as you are and will love you as I do, in spite of yourself."

And God created a new animal to be a companion for Adam. And it was a good animal. And God was pleased. And the new animal was pleased to be with Adam and he wagged his tail. And Adam said, "Lord, I have already named all the animals in the Kingdom and I cannot think of a name for this new animal."

And God said, "No problem! Because I have created this new animal to be a reflection of my love for you, his name will be a reflection of my own name, and you will call him DOG."

And Dog lived with Adam and was a companion to him and loved him. And Adam was comforted. And God was pleased. And Dog was content and wagged his tail.

After a while, it came to pass that Adam's guardian angel came to the Lord and said, "Lord, Adam has become filled with pride. He struts and preens like a peacock and he believes he is worthy of adoration. Dog has indeed taught him that he is loved, but perhaps too well."

And the Lord said, "No problem! I will create for him a companion who will be with him forever and who will see him as he is. The companion will remind him of his limitations, so he will know that he is not always worthy of adoration."

And God created CAT to be a companion to Adam. And Cat would not obey Adam. And when Adam gazed into Cat's eyes, he was reminded that he was not the supreme being. And Adam learned humility.

And God was pleased.

And Adam was greatly improved.

And Dog was happy.

And Cat didn't give a hoot one way or the other.

A priest was asked by a politician, "Name one thing the government can do to help the church."

The priest replied, "Quit making $1 bills."

A little girl became restless as the pastor's sermon dragged on and on. Finally, she leaned over to her mother and whispered, "Mommy, if we give him the money now, will he let us go?"

A Catholic golfer is in a competitive match with a friend, who is ahead by a couple of strokes. The golfer says to himself, "I'd give anything to sink this next putt."

A stranger walks up to him and whispers, "Would you give up a quarter of your sex life?"

The golfer thinks the man is crazy and that his answer will be meaningless, but he says, "Sure." He sinks the putt.

Two holes later the man mumbles to himself, "Boy, if I could only get an eagle on this hole."

The same stranger comes up and says, "Would it be worth another quarter of your sex life?"

The golfer shrugs and again says, "Sure." He makes the eagle.

Down to the final hole. The golfer needs a hole-in-one to win. Sure enough, the stranger moves to his side and says, "Would you be willing to give up the rest of your sex life to make this?"

This time the golfer is more emphatic: "Certainly," he says. The ball goes straight from the tee into the hole.

On the way back to the clubhouse, the stranger walks alongside the man and says, "You know, I've really not been fair with you, because you don't know who I am. I'm the devil, and from now on you will have no sex life."

"Nice to meet you," says the golfer. "My name's Father O'Malley."

DID JESUS LAUGH?

One of the early titles considered for this little book was "Catholic LOL." That's 21st-century technospeak for "laughing out loud."

Laughing out loud is something we probably don't do often enough. That's a reputation Christians in general and we Catholics in particular have earned, especially regarding our faith.

This longstanding image of a dour believer is based in an incomplete understanding of Scripture and tradition. There was once, apparently, even a church rule that forbid any words from the pulpit that might evoke laughter in the congregation. Thank God, we've moved away from that.

Though we've hardly moved far enough.

It's all rooted in a question that for too long has seemed rhetorical: Did Jesus, the Christ, the savior of the world, the King of Kings, the Alpha and the Omega, ever laugh?

Laughter—in particular, Jesus laughing—is something not immediately apparent in Scripture. The Bible is replete with stories of Jesus displaying many emotions. Every Scripture student knows this trivia question: "What's the shortest verse in the Bible?" It's John 11:35: "Jesus wept." But Jesus also mourns. He's angry. He chides. He cajoles. He shows almost every possible human face.

Apparently missing is the image of Jesus the jokester.

In our understanding of familiar Bible stories, Jesus seems to come across as a pretty straight-laced guy. His sermons don't offer an opening monologue like Jay Leno or David Letterman. He doesn't scatter cutesy puns among his comments (at least ones that we easily recognize). Jesus is profound, to be sure. He's pointed. He's prophetic. He's a reflection of God's love. He's instructive, merciful, indignant.

But he's not FUNNY. We don't hear tales of Jesus kicking back with his best buds and sharing a humorous story over a beer.

Or do we?

What does a biblical scholar have to say about all that?

"Is there humor in the Bible? Oh, yes!," said Passionist Father Donald Senior who ought to know.

In addition to being a long-serving president of Catholic Theological Union, Chicago, Senior is a past president of the Catholic Biblical Association of America, the general editor of *The Bible Today*, and author or co-editor of several books about Scripture. In 2003 Pope John Paul II appointed him to the Pontifical Biblical Commission.

There is throughout the Bible, Senior said, an "appreciation of incongruity and appreciation of human foibles…and some very famous stories that I think are filled with humor."

Senior ticked off several, including the tale of Abraham bartering with God over the fate of the people of Sodom (see Genesis 18). "Here we have the God of the Universe bartering with Abraham and Abraham is whittling him down. I can't imagine that that wasn't a funny story for the people of Israel."

There's more, of course.

For instance, Abraham finds it humorous when God tells him—an old, old man—that his equally old wife Sarah will bear him a son and that descendents will be as numerous as the stars in the sky. What's Abraham's response? He "throws himself down and laughs," said Senior. Sarah laughs too when she overhears the angelic strangers say she'll bear a child (see Genesis 18).

But it's in the New Testament where hyperbole, irony and wit really shine. "The parables are just loaded with humor," said Senior.

Biblical scholars have often noted Jesus' "appreciation for the rogue," he said, citing the stories of the wicked manager, the merciless servant and the widow's battle with the unjust judge. "Here's Jesus," said Senior, "a man of stature and integrity, and he appreciates the rogue instead of being so deadly moralistic."

The parables are filled with exaggeration, with things "not meant to be taken literally or seriously…but exaggerated to make a point. I think it's hyperbole meant to provoke a kind of humor; it is a style of humor," said Senior.

"Jesus is not a philosopher; he's telling stories drawn from ordinary life, and it often comes across slightly exaggerated." What's amazing, he said, is that throughout the parables how little Jesus talks directly about God. "The focus is always on some human experience that reflects the divine in some way."

Jesus used humor without necessarily being a joke-teller. "He was a person who had a great love and appreciation of the human condition and humor is certainly part of that. There is a sense of humor in Jesus' stories…and he used it to get peoples' attention," said Senior.

Sort of how any great preacher uses it, right?

So, let's ask again: did Jesus, the Light of the World, the Lamb of

God, the high priest forever, the root of David, ever laugh, guffaw, howl with delight?

Or at least snicker a little?

Well, if he didn't, he wasn't human. And that would be a heresy.

In the early church, Docetism was a heresy that claimed Christ was not both human and divine. Rather, Jesus only "appeared or seemed to appear" to be human. If that were true, we might excuse his lack of humor, but happily the church stuck with the belief that Jesus is "fully human and fully divine."

"Happily" because that—if nothing else—torpedoes any thought that Jesus wasn't given to guffaws now and then.

We just have to look for them.

Besides, if Jesus was as dreary as we sometimes seem to consider him, he'd hardly have been invited to as many parties as he was.

We know Jesus didn't hunker down in a corner during those parties (the equivalent, perhaps, of a neighborhood get-together or barbecue today). He's always in the middle of the action, talking, encouraging celebration, and even turning water into wine to liven up the place a bit. He was, said Senior, "a person of warmth and empathy."

We don't know for certain what little "bon mots" (literally, clever sayings or witticisms) Jesus might have tossed into the conversation, though we can figure out a few. Nor do we know, exactly, what little jokes he might have told, if any.

But we do know that Jesus and other aspects of faith star in a lot of jokes today, some irreverent, others not at all. But most pretty darn funny. OK, before we get too heavy here, it's time for one last Catholic joke before we say goodbye.

The good monsignor was known for two things: his piety and his struggle to play decent golf. One beautiful Sunday morning, instead of going to the parish, he turned everything over to the associate pastor and headed for the golf course.

Watching all this were Jesus and St. Peter. "He should be punished," sniffed St. Peter. "OK," Jesus said, "watch this." The priest's first tee shot sailed onto the green for a birdie. For the rest of the round, the priest played better than he ever had.

"I thought you were going to punish him," said St. Peter. "Keep watching," Jesus told Peter. Then, teeing off on the 18th, the priest nailed a hole-in-one.

Peter was peeved. "This is punishment?" he demanded.

But Jesus just smiled and replied: "So, who can the good monsignor ever tell?"

ABOUT THE AUTHORS

Deacon Tom Sheridan is a veteran writer and editor. In addition to a long career at the *Chicago Sun-Times*, he is also the former editor and general manager of publications for the Archdiocese of Chicago. He was ordained a deacon in 1979 for the Diocese of Joliet (Illinois) and the author of several other books including *Through a Father's Eyes* (Liguori), *Small Miracles – The Extraordinary Stories of Ordinary People Touched by God* (Zondervan), *Mary Miraculous, The Gift of Baptism,* and *The Gift of Godparents* (all ACTA Publications). Deacon Sheridan is now retired and lives in Florida with his wife, Kathy.

Father Gregory Sakowicz has been the pastor of St. Mary of the Woods Catholic Church on Chicago's northwest side and St. Mary's Catholic Church in Evanston and is presently the rector of Holy Name Cathedral. For many years, he has hosted a weekly radio program, "The Catholic Community of Faith," on Relevant Radio (950 AM in Chicago) and has been a regular presider on the televised "Sunday Mass at Mercy Home" on WCIU-TV. He has also appeared on WGN-TV and WLS-TV through the Office of Radio and Television of the Archdiocese. Father Sakowicz was ordained a priest in 1979 for the Archdiocese of Chicago.

Also Available from ACTA Publications

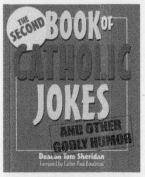

The Second Book of Catholic Jokes

Deacon Tom Sheridan
Foreword by Fr. Paul Boudreau

96 pages, paperback

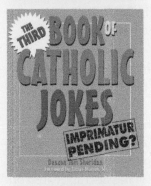

The Third Book of Catholic Jokes

Deacon Tom Sheridan
Foreword by Fr. James Martin, SJ

96 pages, paperback

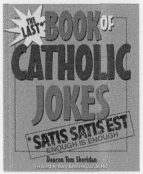

The Last Book of Catholic Jokes

Deacon Tom Sheridan
Foreword by Mary Kathleen Glavich, SND

96 pages, paperback

www.actapublications.com 800-397-2282